D1460446

This book belongs to:

The Mystery of the Whale on the Lake

Written and Illustrated by M. J. Perez

The Mystery of the Whale on the Lake

Written and Illustrated By M. J. Perez

Published By
The Whale on the Lake, LLC
North Canton, Ohio

For permission requests or correspondence, please contact:
The Whale on the Lake, L.L.C.
6545 Market Avenue N. STE 100
North Canton, Ohio 44721
Email at thewhaleonthelakellc@gmail.com

ISBN   979-8-9885667-1-7   (paperback)
ISBN   979-8-9885667-2-4   (hardcover)
ISBN   979-8-9885667-0-0   (e-book)

Library of Congress Control Number: 2023911709

First Edition
The Map of the Whale on the Lake is inspired By the Beautiful Shores of the Counties of the Wonderful State of Ohio and Hand Painted By M. J. Perez
Story By M. J. Perez
Front and Back Book Covers By M. J. Perez
Illustrations By M. J. Perez
Book Designed By M. J. Perez
Edited By M. J. Perez
Technical Support By J. G. P. III
Proofreading Assistance By L. J. P.
2023

For My Son and Daughter. You two are each half of my heart!
For My Husband. Thank you so much for all of your support!
Without the three of you, this book would not be possible. Thank you! I love you!

"Joe! Joe!" Lily exclaimed as she burst through her older brother's bedroom door. Lily was supposed to knock first, but this matter seemed far too important.

"What's up, Lily?" Joe asked. He could tell his little sister was excited about something.

"I heard Mommy and Daddy talking in the kitchen," Lily explained. "I heard them say there's a whale on the lake. Is that true? Have you ever seen a whale on the lake?"

"A whale?!" Joe looked puzzled as he thought about what his sister was telling him. "Are you sure you heard right? I've been going to the beach my whole life. I've never seen a whale once.
Besides, I'm pretty sure whales don't live in any lakes, not even this one."

"What else could they have meant, Joe?" Lily wondered.
"And, where *do* whales live if they don't live in lakes?"

Joe thought for a moment. "Whales live in the oceans. I don't know what Mom and Dad meant. Don't worry though. We'll find out together. We should be able to find out everything we need to know at the library. We'll ask Mom and Dad if we can go."

"Yeah! We can go to the library. Let's find out together!" Lily giggled, excitedly. Joe led the way with Lily skipping behind him to ask their parents if they could all go to the library. There, they would be able to read all about whales and lakes.

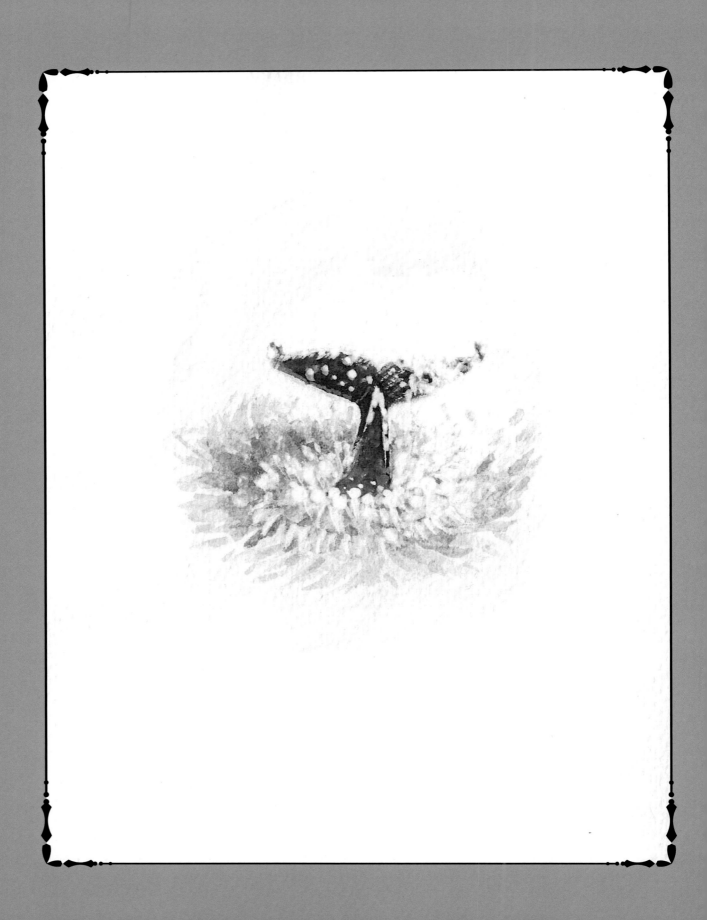

At the library, Joe and Lily were pointed in the direction of books about whales. After choosing a handful of books and finding a table to sit, they searched for answers.

Together the siblings learned whales only sleep for a few minutes at a time. Some whales can sometimes live for hundreds of years!

And, just like Joe said, whales live in the ocean.

Next, Joe and Lily looked for books about lakes.
The pair picked a couple to take back to their table to read.

Together they learned they live on the coast
of one of the smallest of the
Great Lakes.

Lakes are freshwater, not salt water like the oceans.
None of the books about lakes mentioned anything about whales, only walleye.

Joe and Lily learned a lot of interesting things about whales and lakes. The siblings didn't find what they were looking for but did find they always enjoyed their time at the library together.

Fun times are always to be had when the family makes a stop at the city's beach. On a clear, sunny day like today, you can see all the way across the lake.

The tall monument, reaching out towards the clouds from the chain of lake dwelling islands, is quite visible and almost seems to wave 'hello' out on the horizon.

Standing together on the waters' edge, the pair watched the waves splash toward them. Each curling their toes in the sand as they carefully search the waters.

The sun reflected on the surface in blinding shimmers. In the distance, sailboats rode the breeze. The big boat could be heard blowing its horn in the distance. Likely leaving the nearby docs to take its passengers on one of its many daily trips to and from the islands.

A few feet from the brother and sister, a group
of seagulls squawk at each other on some rocks each intended to claim as their own.

"I know we read at the library that we wouldn't see any whales on the lake. I was still hoping we would catch a glimpse. I don't see any whales, though, do you?" Lily asked her brother.

"No," Joe sighed in disappointment. "I don't see any but I was hoping."

"Do you think maybe there's a chance they're just in a different part of the lake, Joe? I don't know what else Mommy and Daddy could have been talking about."

"I don't know, Lily. Maybe. I know this lake isn't the biggest lake but, it is bigger than what we can see. So, I suppose it's possible. Don't worry, Sis. Whatever they meant, we're going to find out."

Joe and Lily's parents announced it was time to leave the beach. Gathering up their shoes, the four dusted sand off their legs and feet before climbing into their seats. Not expecting to see any whales didn't stop them from curiously watching the waves as the family car pulled out of the parking lot and turned towards the grocery store.

Watching the lake rush across their view was like
watching a silent movie set on fast forward. Still no whales in sight.

The grocery store, located across the street from the lake, is lined with huge picture windows. Those giant windows provide the store employees and customers with a great view of the lake.

With such a wonderful view, if there is a whale to be seen, surely the store employees have seen it.

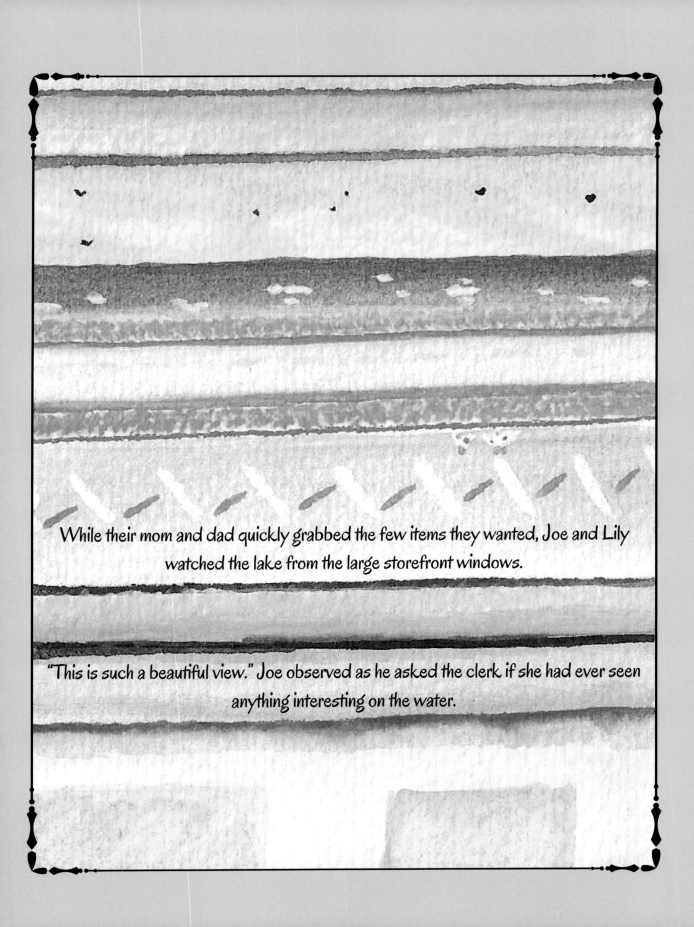

While their mom and dad quickly grabbed the few items they wanted, Joe and Lily watched the lake from the large storefront windows.

"This is such a beautiful view." Joe observed as he asked the clerk if she had ever seen anything interesting on the water.

The store clerk chuckled.

"Yes, I have one of the best views in town, in my opinion! I enjoy seeing all the geese, seagulls and cranes. Along with the many other colorful birds that visit us every year. Sometimes, I even catch a glimpse of one of the bald eagles that nests nearby."

"But what about *whales*?" Lily cheerfully interrupted.

The store clerk sighed with a smile. "No. No whales around here, I'm sorry. That certainly would be a fantastic sight, though. Wouldn't it?"

It was getting late. The sun was setting. Joe and Lily's parents paid for their items while listening to their conversation. Goodbyes echoed through the entryway as the four ushered out through the automatic doors to the parking lot. After walking the short distance to the car, they loaded their groceries then themselves.

From the backseat, Joe and Lily watched the low sun splash sparkles across the lake while vibrant streaks of pinks and oranges painted the sky. The family would go home without the pair finding the answers they spent the day looking for.

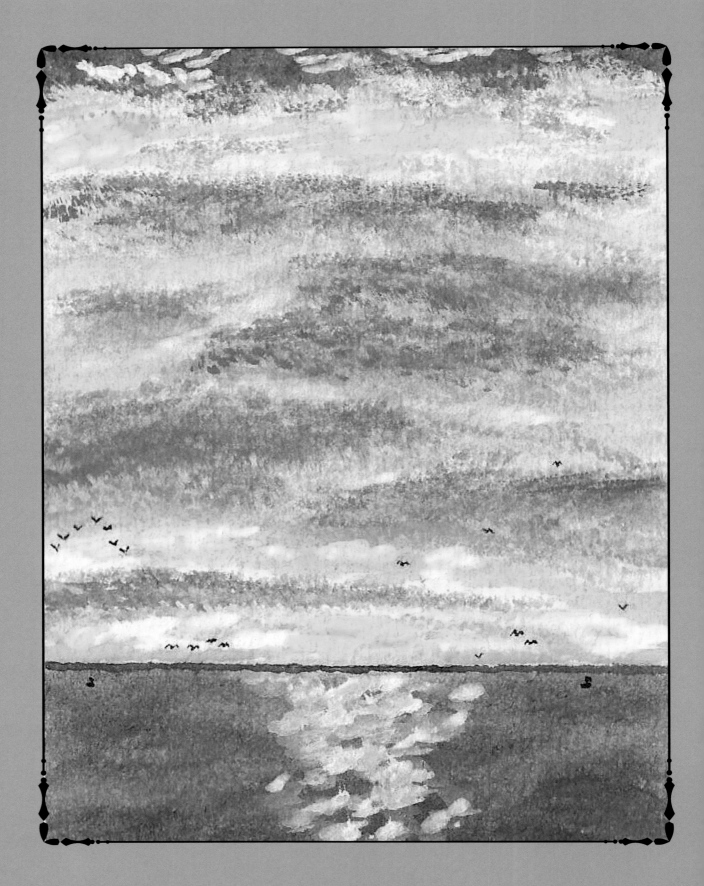

Later at home, Joe and Lily happily thought about their day.

Together, they read books, searched the waves and talked to people they met while out with their parents.

The two had a fantastic day. But, brother and sister were no closer to finding the answer than when they started. There was nothing left to do except ask their parents.

Joe and Lily decided it was time to go do just that. So off the pair went to ask about this mysterious whale living in the lake.

"Daddy," Lily said as she and her brother marched up to their unsuspecting parents. "Whenever you go to work to make the safety rocks, do you see the whales when you drive past the lake?"

Lily's Dad laughed heartily! His daughter's question caught him by surprise. "It's not *safety rocks*, Bug. It's securock. Like *secure rock* except it's one word. And no. I don't see any whales when I drive by the lake. I do see swans and geese, though. Sometimes I even see deer running through the trees. Why do you ask if I see any whales?"

"Well, I heard you and Mommy talking about the whales that live in the lake. I told Joe about it. He's been helping me look all day! But we haven't seen any whales. I want to see the whales, Daddy."

Joe and Lily's dad thought for a few moments. He then smiled and pulled a folded piece of paper out of his pocket.

Carefully unfolding the square, he showed it to the curious duo.

"What your mom and I were talking about was that we live in a place shaped like a whale. Your mom said we live on the whale on the lake."

Joe and Lily gazed thoughtfully at the paper their dad held up for them to see.

On the paper was a painting of the area the family of four calls home. A painting of a map of the counties of northern Ohio that border the shores of Lake Erie.

"Look here." Their dad said, pointing at a spot on the map. Moving their eyes to where he pointed, the two saw it. The county, where the family lives, looks just like a whale!

"Wow!" Joe smiled wide. "I never noticed that before. That's so cool. I guess there was no whale to find *in* the lake, Lily. That's ok, though. We still had lots of fun looking together, huh! To think, this whole time, we're living *on* the whale on the lake!"

Lily rolled with laughter with her brother. "Yeah, Joe, I really did have so much fun with you today! I guess I misunderstood what I heard Mommy and Daddy say. That's so silly. I'm still glad we got to have all that fun, anyway."

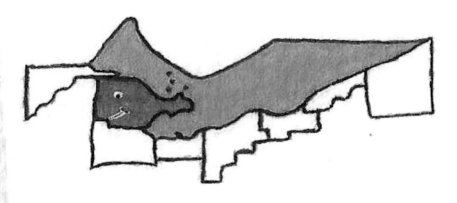

Lily grinned ear to ear as she exclaimed to Joe,
"We live in the most beautiful place ever here on the whale on the lake!
And Mommy said,
'There's no lake life living quite like living on the whale on the lake!'"

The End.

This book is a gift from:

Printed by BoD™in Norderstedt, Germany